The Reggae Scene

The Stars ♪ The Fans ♪ The Music

Peter Manuel and Daniel T. Neely

Enslow Publishers, Inc.
40 Industrial Road
Box 398
Berkeley Heights, NJ 07922
USA

http://www.enslow.com

Peter Manuel, PhD, is a professor of music at John Jay College and an expert in Caribbean music. Daniel T. Neely has a PhD from New York University. He specializes in Jamaican music.

Library of Congress Cataloging-in-Publication Data

Manuel, Peter, 1952–
  The reggae scene : the stars, the fans, the music / Peter Manuel and Daniel Neely.
     p. cm. — (The music scene)
  Includes bibliographical references and index.
  Summary: "Read about the music, stars, clothes, contracts, and world of reggae music"—Provided by publisher.
  ISBN-13: 978-0-7660-3400-6
  ISBN-10: 0-7660-3400-3
  1. Reggae music—History and criticism—Juvenile literature. I. Neely, Daniel. II. Title.
  ML3532.M36 2009
  782.421646—dc22

                     2008048014

Printed in the United States of America

10 9 8 7 6 5 4 3 2 1

To Our Readers:

This text has not been authorized by the musicians or bands mentioned throughout this book.

   We have done our best to make sure all Internet addresses in this book were active and appropriate when we went to press. However, the author and the publisher have no control over and assume no liability for the material available on those Internet sites or on other Web sites they may link to. Any comments or suggestions can be sent by e-mail to comments@enslow.com or to the address on the back cover.

♻ Enslow Publishers, Inc., is committed to printing our books on recycled paper. The paper in every book contains 10% to 30% post-consumer waste (PCW). The cover board on the outside of each book contains 100% PCW. Our goal is to do our part to help young people and the environment too!

Cover Photo Credit: Getty Images
Interior Photo Credits: Alamy/I4images-music-1, p. 18; Alamy/Mark Bassett, p. 33; Alamy/bilderlounge, p. 38; Alamy/RubberBall, p. 39; Alamy/Marwood Jenkins, p. 41; AP Photo/Keystone/Georgios Kefalas, p. 2; AP Photo/Jeff Christensen, p. 5 bottom; AP Photo/Michael Caulfield, p. 9; AP Photo/Mel Evans, p. 27 left; Corbis/Michael Ochs Archives, p. 5 top; Corbis/Lynn Goldsmith, p. 15; Corbis/Shemetov Maxim/ITAR-TASS Photo, p. 28; Getty Images/Tim Graham, p. 8; Getty Images/Frank Micelotta, p. 11 left; Getty Images/Missy Fu, p. 12; Getty Images/Mat Szwajkos/Getty Images for Epic Records, p. 21; Getty Images/Chuck Krall/Michael Ochs Archives, p. 34; Getty Images/David Redfern/Redferns, p. 36; iStockphoto.com/Winston Davidian, p. 4; iStockphoto.com/MBPHOTO, p. 30 (record); Landov/Tim Holt/Photoshot, p. 1; Landov/Luc Gnago/Reuters, p. 10; MPTVIMAGES.COM/Richard E. Aaron, p. 6; Retna Ltd./Wes Orshoski, p. 27 right; Retna Ltd./Youri Lenquette/Dalle, p. 37; UrbanImage.tv Photo Archive, pp. 11 right, 23, 24, 30; UrbanImage.tv/Johnnie Black, p. 16; UrbanImage.tv/56 Hope Road Music/Adrian Boot, p. 25; UrbanImage.tv/Adrian Boot, pp. 31, 35; UrbanImage.tv/David Katz, p. 40.

Cover: Damian Marley performs in Las Vegas in 2006.
Title page: Roots reggae legend Jimmy Cliff plays in London in 2006.
Right: Jamaican reggae artist Shaggy sings to a crowd in Switzerland.

Contents

Reggae was born in the Caribbean nation of Jamaica.

1 Hot Stuff

Jamaica is a land of contrasts. This island in the Caribbean Sea has sparkling beaches, villages nestled in green mountains, bustling city streets—and gritty shantytowns. Most Jamaicans are descendants of Africans taken to Jamaica to work on sugar plantations. Jamaica is not a wealthy country, but it has given the world a wonderful gift: reggae music.

Bob Marley is a worldwide reggae icon. Here, he sings at the Roxy Theatre in Hollywood in 1979.

From Marley *to Dancehall*

Reggae is a big sound from a small island. From the soulful ballads of *Bob Marley* to the dance tunes of *Beenie Man*, reggae has enriched the global music scene. Clubs everywhere throb to the beat of *Sean Paul* hits such as "We Be Burnin'" and "Get Busy."

Dancehall artist Sean Paul gets the crowd excited at Madison Square Garden in New York City.

Peter Tosh and Mick Jagger blended reggae and rock in the early 1980s.

Flavorful *Blends*

Reggae and American music have always gone together well. In the 1960s, Bob Marley started out doing cover versions of rhythm 'n' blues songs.

Today's dancehall DJs look for new trends in hip-hop to use in their own music. But since it began around 1970, reggae has had its own unique sound. It has inspired top international performers to get involved in the scene. For example, one of blues guitarist *Eric Clapton*'s biggest hits was his version of Marley's "I Shot the Sheriff." Top singers and rappers, from *Mick Jagger* to the *Notorious B.I.G.*, have recorded with Jamaican vocalists.

World *Beats*

As West Indian communities in the United States continue to grow—and as the whole world tunes in to YouTube, iTunes, and MTV—Jamaica's music gets more international every year. Teenagers from all over the world are learning to do new reggae dances like Nuh Linga and Gully Creeper.

Fans enjoy an outdoor music performance in Trenchtown, Jamaica.

2 "I'm Your Biggest Fan!"

Fans listen to today's reggae—which is called dancehall—both in the streets of Jamaica's capital, Kingston, and in the fanciest dance clubs of Europe and the United States. Dancehall's true home is the "yard." The yard means any Jamaican home, from a small country village to a gritty urban neighborhood.

In the Yard

On weekend nights, yards throb with music from huge speakers. The music is so loud that you can hear it from a mile away. You can feel it vibrate in your chest. Vocalists— who are called DJs—sing in a thick local dialect called patois (pronounced "patwa"). Patois can be pretty hard to follow for English speakers in other places. In Jamaica, people come to hear the music, to see friends, to meet people, and to dance.

One of the most famous "dancehall queens," or reggae dance stars, is Junko Kudo, from Japan.

A Universal Language

Dancehall's lyrics might be hard to understand, but its beats are so sweet that young people around the world have fallen in love with this music. First, Jamaicans living in places like New York City and London introduced their neighbors to the sounds. Then the tunes got spread by the Internet, clubs, and radio stations. Reggae fans can be found everywhere.

Reggae fans come in all ages and sizes.

3 *Ultimate Style*

For many fans, reggae is not just a music and dance form. It influences ways of dressing, talking, and even thinking. When the roots reggae of *Bob Marley* and others hit the scene around 1970, the songs were about the "sufferers"—the urban lower classes—and spirituality. Casual clothes, like jeans and a T-shirt, were most common.

Rastas

Soon, reggae also became linked with Rastafari. This Jamaican religion started around 1930. Rastafari encouraged black West Indians to reject the people who had enslaved them. Jamaican Rastas (Rastafarians) had a vision of Africa as the promised land.

Rastas disagreed with the common idea that short, straight hair was good and long, kinky hair was bad. They proudly grew their hair in waist-long, curly dreadlocks. This style reminded them of a powerful lion's mane, or of the hair that gave the Biblical figure Samson his strength.

Dreadlocks, or dreads, can be worn loose or wrapped up in the red, gold, black, and green colors of the Rasta flag. These dreads belong to singer David Hinds.

Adding
Some Glitz

The Rasta look is still common in reggae culture. In the 1980s, though, a more popular style emerged. The new style was about wealth, money, and hot fashion trends. Performers such as *Elephant Man* (left) wore artsy clothing and plenty of "bling"— gold necklaces and other glitzy jewelry. Girls put extra effort (and extra money) into custom-made, showy outfits so they could "strut their stuff" on the dance floor.

A dancehall girl adds some glamour to her look with a sparkly wig.

11

Reggae music just makes you want to move.

4 Dance!

With a name like dancehall, this music had better be all about dance! Some people might shake and shuffle in their own way. Usually, though, dancehall has its own special set of dances.

New dances become popular, rule the clubs for a few months, and then go out of style.

The Moves

All the dances have names—like Dutty Wine, Bogle, Pedal and Wheel, and Willie Bounce. Many of them involve imitating actions. For example, Signal the Plane means you light up your cell phone and wave it around. Internet means you move your fingers as if you're typing. When you Buttafly, you flap your legs like wings. Mock the Dread involves waving your hair around like a Rasta. But these dances are already out of date—and new ones are hitting the dance floors every day.

Get with the Program

Some reggae dances go with a particular song. Dancers learn the dance by copying the video or by imitating other fans at clubs. So when the DJ at a club plays **Elephant Man**'s "Pon de River, Pon de Bank" ("Upon the River, Upon the Bank"), boys and girls form a line and do the dance together. The song's lyrics tell them to do moves like sticking their feet in and out of water.

⑤ *On the Road*

Few people realize exactly how much hard work and preparation go into a concert or a tour.

"Pure Magic"

Take singer and producer **Lee "Scratch" Perry**. Perry is one of the reggae scene's most creative personalities. His tours with the New York-based group **Dub Is A Weapon** show a very high musical standard. But keeping to these standards means lots of work. **Dave Hahn**, the leader of Dub Is A Weapon, says, "When you get to perform night after night with one of your musical heroes, it's an amazing experience. But I really need to be on my toes to make sure . . . the band matches up with the vibration that Scratch is going for. It can be hard to make this work, but when it does . . . it is pure magic!"[1]

Offstage

Hahn takes care of the action on the stage, but a lot more happens behind the scenes. Historian, producer, and artist manager Herbie Miller explains, "Touring is not only the fantasy or the spectacle of a performance. The industry offers many work opportunities even if you're not a player of instruments or a singer—behind every successful tour there is a ton of planning . . . that goes on."[2] Lighting, sound engineers, and stage managers play a crucial role in putting on a good show. They are one reason that artists look and sound as good as they do.

Lee "Scratch" Perry takes his act on the road in Aspen, Colorado, in 2007.

The sounds, sights, and smells of a live reggae concert keep fans coming back for more.

6 Live!

Musical events in Jamaica are loud. You don't have to be near a concert to get a sense of the volume. The music can often be heard for miles. Move closer, and the music's intensity increases. It mixes with the sight of people dressed to impress, the smells of cooking food, the blaring of car horns, and the shouts of street vendors. Finally, it can't get any louder, and you're absolutely drowned in sound. There really is no way to prepare for dancehall's chest-shaking volume or powerful bass beats.

Sound Systems

Some of the best-attended live events are sound system dances. At these events, DJs known as selectors take turns spinning records. The selectors compete as people listen or dance the night away. At the end of the night, the best of the night's selectors take turns going "tune fe tune" (trading tune for tune) until—with the crowd's help—a winner is declared. Two of the best sound systems are **Killamanjaro** and **Stone Love**.

Stage Shows

Stage shows are also very popular. Groups of singers take turns performing in front of a band hired to back them all. These kinds of shows can test a band's endurance and song knowledge. Groups like **Grub Cooper's Fab Five** and **We The People Band** are known to keep stage shows interesting. Many of these events go all night long!

Ear Candy

One of the best places to hear reggae is on the radio. Most major cities in North America and Europe have a radio station that plays dancehall. Many of these stations are based at colleges and universities. XM Radio also has a reggae station, hosted by famed music historian Dermot Hussey.

Reggae DJ
Ras Kwame

Island Sound Waves

In Jamaica you can hear reggae on the radio all the time. The most popular stations there include Radio Jamaica, Hot 102, and Irie FM, Jamaica's first 24-hour reggae station. Radio personalities like Richie B, G. T. Taylor, and Elise Kelly make sure people stay up to date on the hottest reggae sounds.

Reggae for Sale

It has never been easier for people to buy reggae. Companies like Trojan Records, Blood and Fire, and Heartbeat Reggae reissue classic songs on CD. Others, like VP Records and Greensleeves, target fans with more modern tastes. These companies allow fans to download songs legally from their Web sites as soon as they are made. Music from all of these companies is also available online through iTunes. This means people in Jamaica and the rest of the world can learn about new releases at the same time.

On the Web

Today, there is plenty of free reggae on the Internet. Many artists create profiles on MySpace and Facebook and post their videos to YouTube. Fans of reggae music also have a strong Web presence. Many fans put up fancy Web sites in support of their favorite artist, record label, or type of reggae.

8 *Hottest Videos*

Most new reggae songs come with music videos that you can watch on YouTube and other Web sites. They aren't always as high-tech or glossy as some MTV videos, but many of them are artful and fun to watch. Some of the videos also give glimpses of life in Jamaica.

Stars on the Small Screen

Many reggae videos have scenes of dancing and partying. **Sean Paul**'s "Get Busy" shows the DJ entertaining people at a lively basement dance. **Elephant Man**, with his bleached hair and ghostly voice, can seem a bit spooky, but most of his songs are about dancing and having fun. In his "Pon de River Pon de Bank" and "Willie Bounce," you can see people doing the dances by those names. On YouTube you can also find Elephant Man's "Dancehall Gym" videos, in which he demonstrates how to do his dance moves.

Love Stories

Other videos are more romantic. They show couples pining for each other, whispering together, and hanging out on beaches and at tropical hideaways. Check out **Tarrus Riley**'s "She's Royal," **Tessanne**'s "Hide Away," and "Always on my Mind" by **Da'Ville** and Sean Paul.

Jamaica Scenes

Finally, several reggae videos show the gritty side of Jamaican urban life. Artists try to give hope to people who struggle to get by in desperate circumstances. **Damian Marley**'s "Welcome to Jamrock" and **Buju Banton**'s "Untold Stories" are especially moving.

Elephant Man and singer Kat de Luna perform on the set of de Luna's video "Whine Up" in Queens, New York.

⑨ *On the Big Screen*

Several important movies—such as the first James Bond movie, *Dr. No*—take place in Jamaica. But no feature film highlighted reggae music until *The Harder They Come* (1973). This movie is about a young man named Ivan, who moves to Kingston from the country to break into the music business. Ivan faces many challenges as he pursues his dream. The film's soundtrack includes music by reggae legends **Cliff**, **Toots and the Maytals**, and **Desmond Dekker**. Both the film and its soundtrack are considered classics. This was the first time that many people outside Jamaica heard reggae.

Rockers

Rockers, another film featuring reggae music, was released in 1978. The film stars drummer Leroy "Horsemouth" Wallace. He buys a motorcycle so he can earn money as a record distributor. His bike gets stolen, and he vows to find it. As he searches, he discovers a crime ring and breaks it up with the help of his friends.

PRODUCED & DIRECTED BY
PERRY HENZELL
Written by Perry Henzell & Trevor D Rhone.

Also starring
CARL BRADSHAW • JANET BARTLEY • RAS DANIEL HARTMAN
WINSTON STONA • BASIL KEANE • BOBBY CHARLTON
An international films release

The Harder They Come was the first major film to feature reggae music and culture.

The cast of *Rockers* is filled with reggae artists—and all of them contributed to the movie's excellent soundtrack.

Dancehall Queen

A more recent reggae film, *Dancehall Queen* (1997), is a sort of Cinderella story. Marcia (played by Audrey Reid) is a street vendor who has trouble making ends meet. When she learns about a dance contest promising a big cash prize, she decides to take a chance and enter. Along the way, she gets a stunning makeover!

11 *Spreading Like Wildfire*

In 1968, a Jamaican music style called reggae came on the scene. The style was known for its laid-back *boom-CHICKA-boom-CHICKA-boom-CHICKA* rhythm. Over this beat, vocalists sang passionately about love, struggle, and the quest for justice.

Marley Hits Home—Globally

The biggest reggae star was **Bob Marley**. His music found its way into the record collections of young people in the United States and Britain. Many people felt that rock music had gotten too commercial. Reggae seemed like a sincere, fresh voice from underground.

More on Marley
Bob Marley was the most famous singer, songwriter, and bandleader of the roots reggae of the 1970s. Marley grew up poor in the slums of Kingston, Jamaica. When he became world-famous, he held on to his spiritual view of life.

British Reggae

In Great Britain, the music took its own direction. West Indians formed hot groups like **Aswad** and **Steel Pulse**. Mixed-race bands

British reggae singer David Hinds performs with his band Steel Pulse.

like the **Specials** spearheaded a "two-tone" movement that joined reggae and rock. Rock stars like **Eric Clapton** and the **Police** worked reggae into their music.

Dancehall Arrives

By 1981, when Bob Marley died of cancer, young Jamaicans were moving on to new music. They followed a new generation of DJs who rapped in a sing-songy style. This style came to be known as dancehall. By the 1990s, dancehall performers like **Buju Banton** had become as popular as Marley had been.

Buju Banton at Jamaica's annual Reggae Sumfest

Beenie Man, known as King of the Dancehall, performs in Moscow, Russia, in 2008.

12 Not So Simple

The term *reggae* covers two different styles of music. The first style is called roots reggae or classic reggae. **Bob Marley** and **Jimmy Cliff** made this style famous in the 1970s. Roots reggae has a laid-back rhythm, soulful melodies, and a rock-style band with electric guitars, bass, and drums. The lyrics might be about love or spirituality.

Evolution

Since the 1980s young people have turned to the dancehall style. Dancehall is closer to rap because the vocals are front and center. But instead of speaking their lyrics, dancehall DJs such as **Beenie Man** sing them in simple tunes on three or four notes. There usually isn't a band. Instead, music comes from a synthesized "riddim" (rhythm) track that is used for lots of songs. The riddims even have their own names, like Pepper Seed, Mad Ants, and Headache.

Most dancehall DJs have colorful names, such as Sizzla, Eek-a-Mouse, Shaggy, Papa San, Lady Saw, Terror Fabulous, and Yellowman.

Praise to the System

Often the music at a club or a dance comes from a sound system instead of a live band. Each sound system has its own equipment, leader, and record collection. The records might include dub plates. On these custom-made records, DJs "big up" (praise) the system. Famous sound systems like **Killamanjaro** and **Stone Love** have been around for decades.

13 *The Studios*

Music is a huge part of Jamaican culture. It is no surprise that Jamaica has many high-quality recording studios. Almost every reggae artist has stopped by *Clement "Coxsone" Dodd*'s Studio One at some point. Most artists have also been to the studio Tuff Gong. *Bob Marley* made his most famous recordings there in the 1970s.

Vinyl Rules

Most of Jamaica's studio recordings still come out as single songs on 7-inch vinyl records. On side one you find the hit single, just as you would hear it on the radio. Side two normally includes an edited version of the same song. Side two's "dub" or "version" might remove the vocals from the recording. This way a

DJ playing the record can talk or sing over the rhythm track, or add sound effects to it.

Today, recording technology is less expensive and more accessible than ever before. Many artists can make professional-sounding recordings at home.

Dubbed Out
Sometimes, studio engineers add so many effects that the dub sounds like a completely different song! In the past, many of these versions were mixed at Lee "Scratch" Perry's Black Ark or King Tubby's Waterhouse Studios.

14 Tale of a Contract

The way to become an international star is to score a record contract. This is a legal agreement between an artist and a recording studio. On records, reggae artists can cross the globe.

Birth of the Wailers

One of reggae's biggest names, singer **Peter Tosh**, grew up very poor. He became famous in a group called the **Wailers** with his friends **Bob Marley** and **Bunny Livingston**. When they started, no one took the Wailers very seriously—except an older musician named **Joe Higgs**.

Higgs took the Wailers under his wing. In 1963, he helped arrange an audition at **Clement "Coxsone" Dodd**'s Studio One. Dodd quickly gave the Wailers a contract. Their first single, "Simmer Down," topped the charts.

Ninjaman's Story

Ninjaman grew up in a rough neighborhood, but he turned his life around. By age twelve, he was DJing with the little-known ***Black Culture Sound System***. Word of his talent spread, and the famed ***Killamanjaro*** sound system hired him.

In 1987, Ninjaman had a big break. He worked with singer ***Courtney Melody*** on "Protection," a major local hit. Producers like ***King Jammy***, ***Henry "Junjo" Lawes***, and ***Gussie Clarke*** took notice. Several record contracts followed. Fans started calling Ninjaman the Don Gorgon, or top DJ.

Ninjaman worked his way to a major career breakthrough in 1987.

Jacob Miller started recording albums in the mid-1970s.

15 Take One!

Have you ever wondered what it's like to make a **record** in a studio? It is more complicated than you might think!

Jacob Miller Makes a Record

Today, singer **Jacob Miller** is considered one of reggae's biggest stars. A close friend of **Bob Marley**, he had a unique vocal style. One of the first records that brought him fame was "Keep On Knocking."

At first, Miller was an up-and-coming singer. Then producer **Augustus Pablo** noticed the young talent. In 1974, Pablo invited Miller to Kingston's Dynamic Studios to make a record.

"Keep on Knocking"

At the studio, Pablo explained what he wanted the musicians to play. After some rehearsal, the rhythm was ready. Miller sang over the rhythm. The studio's engineer made sure that all the equipment worked correctly. Later, Pablo and Miller took the record to **King Tubby**, one of reggae's most creative studio engineers. He mixed a dub version of the song.

Pablo went to a pressing plant and had the record made. This was the usual way to make a record in a studio. But "Keep on Knocking" was a special song. It became a major hit.

At the pressing plant, a studio recording turns into a physical product—a record.

16 *Reggae in Action*

Reggae artists have always dreamed of how to make the world a better place. Many classic songs send out positive messages. Back in the 1960s, "Simmer Down," by ***Bob Marley and the Wailers***, urged "rude boy"—tough, unemployed guys—to stay out of trouble. Jamaicans have a saying, "The half has never been told." They mean that history tends to focus only on rich and powerful people. In songs like

Reggae superstar Peter Tosh showed love for his fans by giving free concerts in poor Jamaican communities. Along with Bob Marley, Tosh was a founding member of the legendary reggae band the Wailers.

"Untold Stories," dancehall DJs like **Buju Banton** tell of the other half of the story. They describe unemployed, poorly dressed teens who spend more money than they earn.

Reaching Out

In the 1970s, singer **Peter Tosh** inspired young people by giving small concerts in poor communities. Since 2001, dancehall DJ **Capleton** has organized and hosted A St Mary Me Come From. This annual performance raises money for Jamaican schools and hospitals.

Protecting What's Timeless

The Jamaica Association of Vintage Artistes and Affiliates (JAVAA) is an organization that helps preserve Jamaica's musical heritage by supporting older musicians. These are only a few ways that reggae artists spread positive messages. There are many more!

Dancehall DJ Capleton brings together fellow musicians to help people in Jamaica.

Do you love reggae music? Become a DJ and spread the word!

17 *Get into It*

There are lots of ways to get involved in reggae music. For most reggae fans, being into the scene means learning the latest dances and doing them with friends. No need for lessons! The moves are simple, and sometimes the song lyrics even tell you what to do. Some students form dance groups that perform in stage competitions at schools and elsewhere.

Juggling Records

Another way to be active is to build up a CD or record collection and become a DJ at parties. Save up your money to get two turntables and a headphone set. Then learn how to cue up records and "juggle"—that is, play several songs on top of the same rhythm.

Make Your Own Music

Perhaps you want to be a reggae singer. Write some lyrics, set them to an original or borrowed tune, and sing them over any rhythm that seems to fit.

You can also try crafting your own rhythms. You might already be used to making your own cell phone ringtones. With computer programs like Garage Band, you can make a catchy rhythm and give it a name. Then you can join the many "beat makers" who exchange ideas on the Internet. Team up with a vocalist, put together a CD, post some samples online, and off you go!

A guitar is your key to learning that favorite Bob Marley tune.

18 For a Living

To have a successful career in Jamaican music, you need to be creative and you need to work hard. Singer and producer **Linval Thompson** fit this description. In the 1970s, Thompson sang on many records that others produced. He had several hit records and worked with **Bunny "Striker" Lee**, one of most Jamaica's important producers.

Reggae legend Linval Thompson

Business *Sense*

Then Thompson started producing his own music. Soon, film and record companies in the United States and Britain began to use his material. Thompson became known internationally as a recording artist and a smart businessman.

Running the System

Sound system owner and operator **Winston Blake** is another smart businessman. As a kid, Blake loved music. One day a family friend suggested that Blake start his own sound system business. Soon Merritone was born. Blake started out by playing music at school dances, churches, and sports clubs. In 1962, he first played in Kingston and got rave reviews. By 1970, Merritone was one of Jamaica's top sounds.

In the early 1970s, Blake expanded his career. He sponsored an amateur talent contest and opened the Turntable Club, one of Jamaica's most important music venues. Merritone is still one of the most important sound system businesses in Jamaica.

Are you interested in working with reggae music behind the scenes? From sound system operator to studio engineer, publicist to manager, photographer to videographer, agent to record executive, there's something for everybody.

Glossary

ballads—Slow, soulful songs that are often about love.

bass—Low musical notes or sounds, or the four-stringed guitar that plays them.

cover versions—Versions of songs that have already been performed or recorded by someone else.

DJs—In reggae, the vocalists who sing or rap over the music.

dialect—A distinct version of a language.

engineers—People who control the recording of a song in a studio. They set up the microphones, set the recording levels, and mix the different sounds.

gritty—Tough, rough, and challenging.

hip-hop—A style of music that usually involves rapping and a strong rhythm.

melody—A musical phrase consisting of a sequence of notes. The melody is usually the part of the song that you remember.

pressing plant—A factory where records are made.

producer—The person who manages and often pays for a music recording.

Rastafari—A West Indian religion that draws some beliefs from the Old Testament and worships Ethiopian emperor Haile Selassie as God.

record distributor—A person or business that advertises records and delivers them to the stores.

recording studios—Places where professional recordings are made.

reissue—To release a record or song that was released earlier.

rhythm 'n' blues—African-American popular music of the 1940s and 1950s, performed by people like Ray Charles and Louis Jordan.

rhythmic—Having a strong, regular beat.

riddim—An instrumental track that is used as a beat (rhythm) for several dancehall songs.

single—A record that features only one song, with another song on the "B" side.

spirituality—An interest in religion or values.

venues—Places where musical events happen.

West Indian—Coming from the English-speaking islands of the Caribbean, including Jamaica, Trinidad, and other islands.

Time Line

1945 Bob Marley is born.

1950–1951 With the release of records produced by Ken Khouri and Stanley Motta, the Jamaican record industry is born.

1950s Sound systems become popular in Jamaica.

1954 Records Limited, Jamaica's first record-pressing plant, is built.

1959 Clement Dodd and Duke Reid begin commercial recording of Jamaican music.

1960 Prince Buster produces "Oh Carolina" by the Folkes Brothers. This is one of the first records to feature Rasta drumming.

1962 Jamaica becomes an independent country; ska emerges as popular music.

1963 The Skatalites form.

1964 The ska song "My Boy Lollipop" becomes a hit in the United States and Great Britain.

1968 Reggae emerges as a new style.

1971 The movie *The Harder They Come* is released.

1972 With the election of the People's National Party (PNP), Jamaica enters a phase of hope; roots reggae becomes popular.

1973 The Bob Marley album *Catch a Fire* becomes an international hit. DJs become popular in Jamaica.

1980 The PNP is defeated, and the mood of Jamaica becomes less hopeful. Dancehall becomes more popular than roots reggae.

1981 Bob Marley dies of cancer.

1985 The release of King Jammy and Wayne Smith's "Sleng Teng" riddim marks the beginning of Jamaica's "digital age."

1987 Peter Tosh, a leading reggae musician, is murdered.

1991 Shabba Ranks, a dancehall vocalist, wins a Grammy Award.

1992 Chaka Demus and Pliers score an international hit with their song "Murder She Wrote."

1995 Shaggy's album *Boombastic* becomes an international hit.

1997 Sizzla releases his breakthrough album *Black Woman and Child*.

2000 Capleton releases *More Fire*, an important Rasta-influenced dancehall record.

2001 The American rock group No Doubt works with Sly & Robbie, Lady Saw, Bounty Killer, and Steely & Clevie on their hit record *Rock Steady*.

2003 JAVAA (The Jamaica Association of Vintage Artistes and Affiliates) is established; the first Passa Passa, a weekly street party, is held.

2004 Sean Paul wins a Grammy for his album *Dutty Rock*.

2007 South African reggae singer Lucky Dube is killed.

2008 Jamaica's minister of culture, Olivia Grange, calls for the creation of a reggae museum; dancehall singer Cocoa Tea releases "Barack Obama," the first of many Jamaican songs recorded in support of Obama's presidential campaign.

2009 Cable channels Reggae Entertainment Television (RETV) and Hype! TV hold their first music video award shows.

End Notes

1. Daniel T. Neely, personal interview with Dave Hahn, August 5, 2008.

2. Daniel T. Neely, personal interview with Herbie Miller, August 6, 2008.

Further Reading

Books

Kallen, Stuart A. *The History of Reggae.* Farmington Hills, Mich.: Lucent Books, 2005.

Miller, Calvin Craig. *Reggae Poet: The Story of Bob Marley.* Greensboro, N.C.: Morgan Reynolds Publishing, 2007.

Moskowitz, David V. *Bob Marley: A Biography.* Westport, Conn.: Greenwood Press, 2007.

Sheehan, Sean, and Angela Black. *Jamaica.* New York: Marshall Cavendish, 2005.

Web Sites

Roots Archives—Database of Jamaican roots reggae albums
<http://www.roots-archives.com>

Riddim Guide—List of riddims and recordings
<http://www.riddimguide.com>

Vintage Boss—Historical perspective on Jamaican music history
<http://vintageboss.blogspot.com>

Index